❧❀ PRAYER ❀☙

The Act of Being with God

❧❲ PRAYER ❳❧

The Act of Being with God

John Killinger

WORD BOOKS
PUBLISHER
WACO, TEXAS

Printed in the United States of America
Library of Congress catalog card number: 81-52524
ISBN 0-8499-0121-9

All Scripture quotations, unless otherwise indicated, are from
The Revised Standard Version of the Bible, copyright 1946, 1952,
© 1971, 1973 by the National Council of the Churches of Christ
in the U.S.A., and are used by permission.

The quotation on pp. 53–54 is reprinted by permission of
Hawthorn Properties (Elsevier-Dutton Publishing Co., Inc.) from
the book,
Christian Meditation: Its Art and Practice, by Wayne Pipkin,
Copyright © 1977 by Wayne Pipkin.

For
SISTER ANASTASIA
with love and gratitude
for all her prayers

❖❨ Contents ❩❖

❖❨ PRAYER ❩❖

The Act of Being with God

⊶❰ Introduction ❱⊷

IF THERE IS ONE SIN that hurts us more than all others, it is surely the sin of not praying. We are meant to live in the Spirit of the Lord—to live joyously, vibrantly, and lovingly in the world. But if we do not pray we cannot live in the Spirit. It is as simple as that. We lack the daily "connection" to God that would make such a wonderful life possible.

How many resources for happiness and power are thus squandered! How many lives never reach the fulfillment intended for them! How much frustration and sorrow there is, even among professing Christians!

And how much poorer the world is because of it!

This is not because people do not believe in prayer. They *do* believe in it. If a poll were to be taken today of all the Christians in the world, it would show an astonishingly high percentage of belief in the power and efficacy of prayer. Nothing has happened to eradicate faith in prayer.

The problem is that people simply do not know *how* to pray. Many do not know the first thing about praying. They do not even know how to begin.

They are like babies given lectures on the glory of walking, and shown movies and slides about the places to which one can walk when one is walking, when what they really need is someone to take them by the hand

and help them put one foot in front of the other. The babies sincerely *want* to walk, but only they know how terribly difficult it is in the beginning.

There are many wonderful books about prayer. Some describe the bliss of the experience of prayer. Others deal with the psychological benefits to the person who prays. Still others treat the more difficult question of intercessory prayer, and how our prayers are helpful to those for whom we pray.

But those are books for the person who already knows how to pray, who has had at least an introduction to the actual experience of prayer and merely needs encouragement to keep at it or some word about refining his or her technique.

This little book is something different.

It is a very basic introduction to what one does when he or she begins to pray.

It assumes that the person reading it really wants to learn how to pray; that he or she really wants to take the first fumbling steps and get the feel of what prayer is all about.

Therefore it is not an attempt to sell you anything.

It is simply a book of suggestions about where to begin.

About *attitude* in prayer.

About *times of the day* for praying.

About *the best place* for prayer.

About *posture*.

About *mood*.

And then about *specific methods* for beginning to pray.

Some of the methods may be ones you have tried before. In that case, you may wish to begin with others.

The point is, this is a book about mechanics. It is a

how-to book—a book written for the novice, the real beginner. The accent is on very practical matters.

If you are already beyond this stage and are looking for something more inspirational, then you would do well to look elsewhere.

Here we are dealing with fundamentals.

❧ An Attitude of Prayer ☙

WHAT DO YOU EXPECT from prayer? Your attitude can make a great difference in the degree of success you have.

As people who know best will tell you, the benefits of prayer rarely come in terms of what you expect when you begin to pray. In that way prayer is like marriage. Its greatest fruits are unimaginable at the stage where one stands before the altar; they come slowly, sometimes imperceptibly, through the years, and even then they are seen most clearly in retrospect, from the point of view of one who savors the memories of them.

This is to say that prayer, like marriage, is an act of faith. You know that it is good, that it is natural, and that it holds promise for you.

In the beginning, that is all you need to know.

Specific expectations can lead to disappointments.

You might expect to become a stronger Christian. But if that is your intention in praying, you will probably find yourself becoming frustrated.

You might expect to gain more power with God, so that you can effectively heal the sick or work other miracles in your environment. Again, if that is your intention, you will be unhappy.

Prayer is not something we engage in because we wish to achieve anything.

Prayer is communion with God. It is the act of being with him. Nothing more, nothing less.

Now a great many things come of this—later on, when you have been at it a while.

But in the beginning that's all it is—being with God.

A great many people are frustrated at prayer because they don't understand this. They see it as some great romantic venture of the soul from which they return as conquering heroes, or as some equally marvelous merit badge contest in which they are given points for every moment they manage to spend in the posture of devotion.

But prayer is so much more simple than that, and so much more substantive.

It is coming into the presence of the One who loves us all the time—more than our parents ever loved us even in the best of times—and waiting in that presence.

That's all. Coming and waiting.

Prayer, you see, is a fellowship.

You don't even have to talk, when you don't want to or don't know what to say. All you have to do is be aware of the fellowship. Pay attention to it, the way you would if you were with an ordinary friend.

Some people never learn to pray because they say they don't know what to say to God. Words are not easy for them.

But you don't *have* to talk to God. He accepts you in silence as well as in words.

All you have to do is feel his love for you, and, when

you feel it, respond in any way your heart wants to respond.

It's really that simple.

Maybe you can see, then, why attitude is important.

You do not pray in order to get something out of God that he was going to give you anyway.

You pray in order to feel his love and to give him yours.

What happens when you do this, of course, is that you begin to see how rich your life already is—how he has surrounded you with more gifts and joys than you were aware of.

But you don't pray in order to achieve something.

You pray in order to be with God.

✦⧏ The Best Time for Praying ⧐✦

ST. PAUL SPEAKS of praying "without ceasing."

It is not as hard as it sounds, really. You merely learn to become aware of God's presence with you all the time, whatever you are doing.

A friend who commutes to work says that he sits and communes with God every time he stops at a traffic light.

You can do it every time you open the refrigerator.

Or when you brush your teeth.

The trick is simply to turn your thoughts toward God at lots of specific times every day.

One way to do this is to practice remembering him while you are performing one specific action all week.

When you are making up the bed, for instance. Or setting the table. Or picking up your mail. Or walking to school.

Then, for the next week, pick another action.

What you will discover is that you remember God when you are doing last week's action, too. And the week's before that. It is a cumulative effect. Soon you will be thinking about God a great deal of the time.

But it is also helpful to have a *special* time each day when you concentrate on being with God.

Nearly all the great saints—those who have mirrored the presence of God in their faces and attitudes—have insisted on this.

It becomes the anchoring time, the one that stabilizes your entire day and centers it on God. Without it, your devotion remains diffuse and unfocused. Without it, you will not really grow in your knowledge of God.

Think of it this way. If there were someone you truly wanted to get to know, to know in a very deep and meaningful way, you would not consider it enough to visit with that person only in the odd moments of your day. You would want to reserve a time when you could sit down with him or her and be together uninterruptedly as you talked and listened to one another. The odd moments would be more valuable than ever in the light of this period of concentration.

It is the same in our relationship to God. We need regular draughts of time for exploration and fellowship.

As for which is the best time of day for this greater effort at prayer, that is a matter you must decide for yourself after considering your daily patterns. People vary in their opinions of the best time for praying, just as they vary in their opinions of the best times for doing others things such as working, exercising, or reading the newspaper. A time that is good for one person may not necessarily be good for another.

What you must do is consider your schedule, reflecting on it carefully, and decide when you could pray best. You might even need to experiment for a few days and see which time or times work better than others.

There are two important things to remember.

First, it is important not to relegate your praying to a time of day when you are too exhausted or distracted to enjoy being in the presence of God.

C. S. Lewis once said that "no one in his senses, if he has any power of ordering his own day, would reserve his chief prayers for bed-time—obviously the worst possible hour for any action which needs concentration."

It might be argued, of course, that if prayer is enjoying the experience of God's loving presence, there is no better time to pray than when one is weary and has exhausted his or her own resources. And in a sense that is correct.

But what kind of husband is it who turns to his wife to give her attention only after he has completely exhausted himself through the affairs of the day and evening? Or what kind of parent reserves for loving his or her child only the moment when he or she sits half in a stupor at the end of a long day?

No, Lewis is right. Bedtime is not the best time for prayer—*unless* you find it to be a time of such inner relaxation and composure that you can concentrate better then on the presence of God than you can at any other available time. And some people *do* seem to be more alert in the evening than they are in the morning.

It is a matter which you must decide for yourself as an individual.

The second important thing about the time you

choose, once you have chosen it, is that you should observe it *faithfully*.

This may be very hard for you, but there is a good reason for it. The reason is that if you don't observe the time strictly you will soon forget to observe any time of prayer at all.

Of course your intentions will be the best. You will say, "I am a busy person, and it does not suit me to designate a particular hour every day when I shall pray. It is practical, in my case, to be more flexible. I shall merely see when I have a slack time during the day, and I will fill that time with my praying."

And you will really mean to do that.

But take it from the master of the flexible schedule—you won't!

You may be faithful to do it for several days, but then one day you will slip and fail to give your attention to prayer. A few days later you will slip again, and before you know it you will have given up on it entirely.

Admit to yourself that it is very difficult to establish the habit of doing something new like praying at a certain time every day. It *is* difficult.

Then go ahead and do it.

In a few weeks it will seem as natural in the course of your day as eating a meal or brushing your teeth.

How long should this daily time of prayer be?

Again, that will depend on you, and on the method or methods of praying you find most useful.

If you combine your prayer with meditation on the scriptures, as some people do, you will require long enough both to study and to "listen" to the scripture passage. A time of simple meditation can obviously be shorter.

It is probably best not to be too ambitious at first, setting a longer time for yourself than you find comfortable and rewarding. Too long a time can cause you to become distracted or discouraged.

You might begin with as little as ten or fifteen minutes. That way you can tuck it into your present schedule without completely disrupting everything.

If you work at a business, you can even slip it into your lunch hour. Many Christian businesspersons make a practice of locking the office door at twelve o'clock, sitting quietly at their desks in prayer for a quarter of an hour, then going off for their luncheon engagements. It is amazing, they say, how this affects the tone and content of their table conversations.

If you keep house, you can guard the few minutes between the time when the kids leave for school, beds are made, and the dishes washed, and the time when you have to go to the market.

If you are a high school student, you can fence off fifteen minutes during a regular study period at school, or at lunchtime, or when you first return home from school.

Make the period relatively short at first, and observe it regularly. Then you will probably find that it has a tendency to grow longer as the weeks and months go by.

That is natural.

When you are first getting acquainted with a new friend, you are aware of a certain awkwardness. It takes a while to break through the "strangeness" barrier. Later, when you know each other very well, and find that you enjoy each other's company, the time seems to fly when you are together!

✦❋ The Best Place for Praying ❂✦

WHERE YOU DO YOUR PRAYING is not an all-important matter. Some people, like the late Frank Laubach, who had a tremendous prayer life, spend much of their time traveling, and so must learn to pray on buses, trains, and airplanes—and in hotel rooms and restaurants.

But having a definite place is helpful in the beginning, just as having a specific time is.

It need not be a fancy place. Jesus told the disciples to go into a room and shut the door and pray there (Matthew 6:6). The kind of room he had in mind was small, because none of the disciples was wealthy, and it was probably very plain, with earthen walls and floor.

Perhaps the two most essential characteristics of a place for praying are, one, that it be quiet, so that you will not be distracted, and, two, that it be moderately comfortable.

Quietness is a must.

True prayer, you will learn, is composed as much of silence as it is of speaking.

Some people are much more adept at "inner silence" than others—at discovering and maintaining an unflappable quietness at the centers of their being, regardless of what is going on around them.

But even the best of us can be readily distracted from communion with God by the sudden ringing of a telephone, the whir of a dishwasher, the buzzer on an electric dryer, or piercing noises from a teenager's stereo set.

It may be, because of this, that you will have to consider the matters of time and place together when deciding where you can pray, in order to have part of your house or apartment to yourself at the time when you sit down to pray.

I have known several persons who got up in the morning before their families in order to have a quiet time and place for their devotional life. This is sometimes necessary, especially in large families.

As for the telephone, it will not hurt to lay the receiver off the hook for the period of your prayers, and then replace it afterwards. Or, in some areas, it is possible to have the telephone company install a silencing mechanism on your phone, so that you can push a little switch and turn off the sound for as long as you like.

The matter of a moderate comfort is also important, especially in the beginning.

This may sound strange if we think of Jesus' long periods of prayer in the wilderness, or the stories of holy persons who have sought refuge for meditation in the desert and in the mountains. But that can come later, if you feel led to do it.

In the beginning, it is better not to be distracted by an unnecessary degree of discomfort. Let God *ask* for such signs of devotion if he wills them. For the moment, concentrate on learning how to pray.

Too much comfort, of course, is not good either. You don't want to be lulled into sleep by lying in a soft bed or sitting in an overly luxurious chair.

Many persons find sitting at a desk or table quite suitable. Housewives often like to sit at the kitchen table, so that they are praying right at the center of where much of their activity occurs. Or, if you prefer to kneel, the bedside or the edge of a rather firm sofa offers a modest prop so that you do not become physically tired or cramped while praying.

There is some reason for using the same place regularly for your prayers. Subconsciously, this creates an expectancy of prayer whenever you return to the place. Just as you expect to enjoy a meal when you sit down at the dining table, or to sleep when you go to bed, you expect to be in communion with God.

Some persons who have had great experience in prayer like to have a special place in the home that is used *only* for prayer. This heightens the sense of expectancy even more.

You can do this very simply, if you feel that it would be meaningful to you. Merely select the portion of a room you wish to use, or a large closet, or a small room, if you have a spare one, and arrange it with such furnishings as you would like to appropriate for your prayer life.

Some persons like to arrange an interest center, with such items as a Bible, a book of meditations, a candle, and a meaningful picture. I know several persons who use pictures or etchings of Christ. Roman Catholic friends often use pictures of the Madonna. I myself prefer a variety of pictures—usually postcards or magazine clippings showing nature scenes, children's faces, poor people's faces, and pictures of bread or other foods. And I change these pictures from time to time.

A few people I know use a *prie-dieu*, a specially made little kneeling bench with a shelf on top for a Bible, a prayerbook, a hymnbook, or whatever other aids to devotion are desired. (The word *prie-dieu* is French, and means literally "pray God.") Such an item of furniture fits unobtrusively into almost any room or office.

Some priests and ministers prefer to have their daily prayers before the altar or communion table of the church, where the bread and wine of the communion remind them more forcibly of the presence of God in their lives through the sacrament. Two ministers of the Church of England, the Dean of Liverpool Cathedral and his assistant, follow this practice, and spread the pages of the daily newspaper on the floor beneath them, where their eyes will be caught by the names of persons for whom they wish to offer prayer.

In the home, you may wish to pray with a bit of bread or wine before you as a kind of "unofficial" sacrament, to remind you of God's loving care for you in the wilderness of life. Or you may prefer, as I do, bread and tea.

These matters are beginning to impinge upon the subject of one's *mood* in praying, and we shall be discussing that shortly.

First we must give a brief consideration to the topic of posture.

❧ Your Posture in Praying ☙

A GREAT DEAL has been said and written in recent years about "body language," and how we express ourselves nonverbally by the various postures of our bodies.

This is reason enough to be concerned about how we compose our bodies for prayer.

The position we assume while praying not only says

something to God; it also sends secret messages to our own subconscious minds which either help or hinder us as we pray.

Actually, of course, prayer never completely depends on bodily attitudes. You can pray effectively while walking along the street, riding in an elevator, standing at a counter, or lying on the flat of your back. But as a general rule there can be no doubt that a humble, reverent pose is most conducive to the spirit of faithful devotion you are concerned to develop in your special prayer time.

Since ancient times, kneeling has in most cultures been considered the most respectful posture for approaching the deity. This was possibly a derivation from the practice of kneeling before the king or tribal authority, who in many cases held the power of life or death over the subject before him.

In the New Testament, we have the picture of Jesus praying in the garden of Gethsemane on the night before his crucifixion, and, according to the description we are given, he "fell on the ground" in prayer (Mark 14:35). The Gospel of Matthew even says that he "fell on his face and prayed" (Matthew 26:39).

This is the only record we have of Jesus' posture in prayer, however, and it is possible that the posture in this instance was dictated at least in part by the anguish of the crisis he was facing. Anyone who has sought the will of God in an agonizing life-decision knows what an appropriate gesture it can be.

Common sense suggests that Jesus did not always pray in a similar position. During his days and nights in the wilderness, he probably prayed sitting down, or even while walking around. We have no record of his ever kneeling to talk to his Father, or teaching that prayer should always be done on the knees.

The disadvantage of kneeling to pray is that kneeling can become a very tiresome posture when continued for very long. Some people, too, are afflicted by arthritis or other problems with their knees, and cannot manage a kneeling position at all.

In most cases, therefore, it is probably better to cultivate the habit of praying in a seated position which will not tire the body and distract you from the important thing you are doing—namely, engaging in communion with God. The body can assume a quiet, reverential pose even when sedentary.

Or, if you wish to use a combination of postures, you can begin your prayers by kneeling, then rise and sit during the major portion of them, and finally kneel again as a final gesture of submission and commitment.

Years ago, when I was more supple, I prayed with such a combination method, and found it very rewarding. I would kneel until my forehead was against the coolness of the floor, remain there a minute until I felt throughout my body the sense of my desire to pray, then rise and pray by my bedside, and complete the praying by returning to the prone position once more. During this final moment I waited until I felt the Lord summoning me to rise, and this always gave me a special sense of completion about my praying.

But again the whole point has to do with "inner devotion," with the posture assumed by the soul itself, and that is not entirely dependent on a regimented position of the body. You will want to discover the posture in which *you* are able to pray comfortably and meaningfully.

✦❐ The Mood for Praying ❐✦

THE MATTER OF *MOOD* in praying is a very intangible and difficult subject to treat, but we should at least consider it.

In a sense, we have been talking about it all along, in discussing the place and time and posture of prayer, for each of these things is able to affect mood.

But now we need to go further and say a word about your inner disposition in praying—how you compose your soul for what you are about to do.

This can be very important.

If you go into prayer with the attitude of "Well, I hate to stop what I am doing and go to my devotions, but I suppose I must," you will find it a lot harder to enter into the spirit of God's presence than if you think, "Oh, good, it is time for me to sit down with God again and feel the renewing power of his love."

The person who is experienced in prayer often describes it as a time of genuine ecstasy, when tides of joy sweep over the exultant soul and the love of the Father seems to wrap around the one praying like a wave or cloud of sensuality, triggering explosions of delight and adoration.

This is the result of spending months and even years at one's prayers.

But it is easier to arrive at such a level of delight later if you can begin to feel it a little very early on, and think of this each time as you go to your devotions. Do not dwell on the fact that prayer is a new enterprise for you, or that it is going a bit slowly, but concentrate on the more positive aspects of the experience.

Did you feel the presence of God with you the last time, even for a moment?

Remember that as you go to your prayers this time.

Did you feel a sense of cleanliness and purity afterwards that clung to your mind for hours like the scent of a nice perfume?

Then think about that as you go to pray now.

Prepare yourself for the joy of praying by *anticipating* the joy it will be.

We do that in other things, don't we? If we are going out to dine in a good restaurant in the evening, we think about it all day long. If we are going to be with a special person for a while, we look forward to our time together, and even dream of what we shall talk about.

Why shouldn't we do the same thing in prayer?

If thinking about the meal we shall eat enhances the dining experience, and dreaming about the person we shall be with prepares us for the excitement of being with that person, then why shouldn't we stimulate ourselves for our rendezvous with God by anticipating the joy and meaning of the meeting?

Some persons actually go through a ritual of preparation before entering their times of prayer.

Carlo Caretto, one of the Little Brothers of Charles de Foucauld, has described how he prepares for early morning prayer.

Arising very early, a long time before daybreak, he goes out into the cold night air of the desert and sits on a hillside, watching the stars. He looks at the various constellations, and meditates on the grandeur of the One who created the heavens and the earth.

Then he comes back into the small hermitage which Père de Foucauld built for himself, where the sanctuary lamp filled with olive oil flickers and casts its light on the earthen walls. Wrapping his *bournous* around him for warmth, he kneels down on the sand before the altar and begins to pray.

Why doesn't he pray out on the hillside, under the stars?

Because, says Brother Carlo, he prefers to come to God before the Eucharist, where God has given himself as bread.

"It is here," he says, "that I have felt the presence of God most strongly; it is here that I have experienced for myself Christ's dramatic recapitulation of the history of salvation.

"And I always come back here when I want to make my way to the threshold of the invisible, because the Eucharist is the surest doorway opening on to it."

But the time under the stars is preparation. It stills the man's soul before he makes his approach.

"We need some moments of preparation," he says, "a little time in which to calm the soul, or to wake it up—a vestige of human prudence, so as not to turn up like brutes for such an exacting task as prayer."

It is in this respect, I think, that we ought to mention fasting.

Not many people today are acquainted with fasting as a religious discipline, but those who are find it to be a very effective way of preparing the self for engaging in prayer.

This need not mean total abstinence from food for a prolonged period. Actually, it can take many forms.

For example, you might decide to eat no meat on a certain day of the week, or to drink nothing but water all day. Or, if you are addicted to sweets and desserts, it could mean forgoing these for a period of time.

The idea is to willfully give up certain things you ordinarily enjoy—it is no sacrifice to forego what you do not like or would not ordinarily have anyway!—as a sign of your desire to follow Christ. In addition to benefitting your body, you are demonstrating your serious intention of living a sober, well-ordered life. And, while such signs are probably not very meaningful to other persons, they can be quite helpful to you in reaching new levels of relationship to God.

Personally, I happen to be partial to other forms of abstinence as a preparation for devotional life, such as abstaining from looking crossly at others for a day, or from speaking grumpily, or from making critical remarks. These, I find, are much more useful ways of honoring God before I come into his presence; and, even if I fail in my inner pledge to live more positively, the confession with which I begin my time of prayer becomes a meaningful basis for relationship between us.

But this is to take nothing away from the practice of spiritual fasting, which has very noble traditions within our faith.

Yet another form of personal preparation for prayer, practiced mostly by Catholic friends, is to make the sign of the Cross on oneself as a confession of obedience to the Christian way.

I once heard a lovely nun, who had been a Protestant and a housewife until she was forty years old, say that she wished her Protestant friends were not so afraid of this simple gesture of relationship to Christ. Even if she were to leave the Catholic church, she said, she would continue to make the sign of the Cross before prayers until she died, for she found the inward dimension of this symbolic action to be exceedingly helpful to her.

The important thing, overall, is to discover some method of preparation which you find useful in your own spirit and personality. It may be the contemplation of nature, as in Brother Carlo's case, or spiritual fasting, or making the sign of the Cross.

Or it might be something entirely different, such as playing a hymn on the piano.

Or sipping a cup of tea.

Or exercising.

Or blanking your mind for a few minutes.

Or listening to a record.

Or reciting a favorite poem.

Or taking a walk.

Or staring at a picture.

Or reviewing the events of the day.

Or writing a single word, such as the word "love," over and over on a piece of paper.

The idea is to create a new mood in which to make your approach to prayer, to draw a line between where you were in the day's activities and where you are going to be when you submit yourself to God's presence. To enter such a new mood you may require nothing except the ready consciousness that that is what you are about to do.

But the important thing is to enter the experience with anticipation and joy, as befits coming into the presence of the Most High and feeling his love and care for you.

* * * * *

From this point on, we shall be talking about actual methods of prayer—ways of thinking or speaking or being before God.

As in everything else we have said, you will wish to seek the method or methods most suitable to your own personality structure. One way of doing this is simply to try one method after another, allowing enough time to get the feel of a method before going on to another. Then, when you have tried them all, you can decide on the one, two, or three methods you would like to use most constantly in your developing prayer life.

❧ The Prayer of Silence ❧

WE BEGIN WITH THE EASIEST and yet the hardest of all prayers—the prayer of silence.

Easiest because the brain is not taxed to think of words to speak to God.

Hardest because most of us are so unused to silence, to waiting, to being still and feeling our souls become still.

Some of us have an absolute aversion to silence. We live in a world of sounds and noises—bleeping sirens, whirring gadgets, pulsating stereos, chattering radios and television sets. If we are left alone for half an hour, we turn on a noise for companionship. We idolize quiet, rustic settings, but even when we go there we take our radios and turntables with us.

Yet from the beginning of time, and in all religions, God is associated with eternal silence. Mystery is hushed. Holiness is awesome, still, unspeakable.

The greatest temples and cathedrals have always been ones that embodied this stillness, not ones that provided excellent acoustical qualities for the transmission of voices. By allowing us to leave the world of sound, they seem to usher us into the presence of the One who has been called "the Wholly Other."

Perhaps the best way to begin praying, then, both when we are first learning to pray and long afterwards, is by coming before God in quietness—by drawing near and waiting in silence, with no anxious straining after words or thoughts.

We are pragmatic, and silence makes us nervous. Nothing seems to be on its way to happening.

No matter. Wait.

Prayer is not "useful" in the sense that certain other things are. We do not get to its benefits directly.

After all, we are not dealing with the butcher or the insurance man or the pharmacist.

We are waiting before the Creator of the World, the Most High God, the Transcendent One, the Alpha and the Omega, the Beginning and the End, the Source of All Holiness.

He is so holy, in fact, that the ancient Jews would never speak his name. Only once a year did the high priest of Israel dare to enter the Holy of Holies and utter it. And, even then, the people tied a rope around his ankle so they could draw him out if he should be struck dead while doing so.

Viewed in that light, what do we have to say to God? What *can* we say?

Reverently, we come before him and kneel or sit in his presence, without speaking.

We concentrate only on what we are doing—waiting in his presence.

We listen to the silence.

Will he speak?

Perhaps.

And if he doesn't?

We listen to the silence.

Without speaking, he sifts us.

Our earthly ambitions are seen to be tawdry, our fears groundless, our resentments self-paralyzing, our hurrying pointless.

Love, peace, joy, gratitude, the fruits of the spirit.

These count.

These take over again in our lives.

We bless his name.

That is what the silence comes to.

The prayer is over, and we return to our work.

But something is different. We don't feel so harried. Our very beings are lifted. His Spirit encradles our own.

Perhaps your heart will beat too fiercely when you try this prayer of silence, and you will want to stop.

Try breathing deeply, and concentrating on that.

Inhale.

Exhale.

Wait before God.

Inhale.

Exhale.

Wait before God.

You will get the trick of it.

Many holy persons in our own tradition, as well as those from the Eastern religions, have employed this technique.

You might even imagine yourself as a young rabbit or a small bird in the hands of God. Your heart is pounding because he is holding you. Your life is in his hands.

But that is getting into prayer with images, which we shall discuss later.

For now, let us only consider a slight variation of silent prayer.

◆C Listening to God's Questions ℈◆

SOME CHRISTIANS have found this to be an effective method of waiting before God. Instead of concentrating on God and the silence, they tune themselves to listen for God's voice in their subconscious minds raising questions for them.

"Here I am, God," they say in effect. "I am trying to give you my attention. What questions do you wish to ask me today?"

Perhaps the inner voice will say, "Who do you love?"

"Why, I love you," the one praying will respond. And then he or she will think, "But I haven't shown it, have I? I have been busy and self-indulgent. I have not honored the commandments."

The answer is modified. "I am sorry, Lord. I *want* to love you."

"Have you forgotten to write to your friend in the hospital?" the voice may ask.

"Oh, I *did* mean to do that, but it slipped my mind. Lord, give her strength for this ordeal. Be with her now. Borrow from my strength and give it to her, Lord; she needs it much more than I."

"What about Joey? Don't you think something is bothering him?"

Thoughtfulness.

Then: "I hadn't thought about it, Lord, but I think you're right. He *has* been moody lately. Teenagers don't have it easy, I guess. Please help him, Lord, whatever it is. And I'll be especially attentive to him today when he comes in."

More silence.

"Do you really love me?"

"Lord, you know I do. Why do you keep asking me that?"

"Then why haven't you done something for that poor family over on Toddington Court—the one whose father has leukemia?"

And on and on it goes.

You get the idea of how it might work for you.

It is an unusually hard and searching kind of prayer, and one that is especially helpful to the development of a thoroughly Christian conscience. Its benefits are often missed when we spend all our prayer time *talking* to God, instead of *listening*.

✦⟪ Using a Single Phrase ⟫✦

THE ANONYMOUS CHRISTIAN MYSTIC of the Middle Ages who wrote *The Cloud of Unknowing* advised using a single word as a prayer thought and saying it over and over.

"God" and "love" were two he suggested.

The idea is to use the word as a kind of mantra that induces a hypnotic effect in the soul. That way it constantly recenters the soul, banishing greed, false ambition, anxieties, fears, and resentment to the periphery of one's life.

"Thine only, thine only," were the words favored by the great Quaker mystic Thomas Kelly.

Kelly also liked to use a phrase from the Psalms, such as "So panteth my soul after thee, O God."

This variation of the method, concentrating on a few words from scripture, has always been popular in monastic orders. Since the early Middle Ages, monks have scoured the pages of the Bible, especially the Psalms and the New Testament, for simple, meaningful phrases which they would memorize and then repeat over and over as simple prayers of the heart.

Consider these parts of verses, and the effect of constantly repeating them in a prayerful attitude:

"The Lord sustains me" (Psalms 3:5).

"O Lord, our Lord, how majestic is thy name" (Psalms 8:1).

"God is our refuge and strength" (Psalms 46:1).

"Fill me with joy and gladness" (Psalms 51:8).

"The Lord is your keeper" (Psalms 121:5).

"I will praise the Lord as long as I live" (Psalms 146:2).

"Blessed are the pure in heart" (Matthew 5:8).

"I will arise and go to my father" (Luke 15:18).

"I am the living bread" (John 6:51).

"In him we live and move and have our being" (Acts 17:28).

"All who are led by the Spirit of God are sons of God" (Romans 8:14).

"Come, Lord Jesus" (Revelation 22:20).

You have but to turn through the pages of the Bible to see that such phrases almost literally leap out at you to be used.

Choose one and use it for a week.

Then choose another the next week, and so on.

All of your life, whenever there is unusual pressure on you or you are facing some crisis or calamity, the phrases you have thus memorized and used as prayers will rise automatically into your consciousness and become holy food, nourishing your heart.

Do not be concerned about their theological meaning. That is not at issue here. Simply repeat them, over and over, until you do so almost unconsciously. At that point, they will begin to do you the most good, for then your spirit will be most yielded to God's Spirit.

Thomas Kelly said that is when God's Spirit takes over and begins to pray through ours, so that we are only blessed channels through which God talks to God:

"We pray, and yet it is not we who pray, but a Greater who prays in us. Something of our punctiform selfhood is weakened, but never lost. All we can say is, Prayer is taking place, and I am given to be in the orbit. In holy hush we bow in Eternity, and know the Divine Concern tenderly enwrapping us and all things within His persuading love. Here all human initiative has passed into acquiescence, and He works and prays and seeks His own through us, in exquisite, energizing life. Here the autonomy of the inner life becomes complete and we are joyfully *prayed through* by a Seeking Life that flows through us into the world of men."

⊹《 The Jesus Prayer 》⊹

"LORD JESUS CHRIST, have mercy on me."

That is what is known as "the Jesus prayer." It is the English version of the Greek phrase *Kyrie eleison* which has been embedded in the liturgies of the church since earliest times.

For centuries, it has been used in the repetitive manner we have been describing. The person praying it simply uses it over and over, like a chant.

Between the years 1851 and 1863, an unknown Russian Christian wrote a book called *The Way of the Pilgrim,* in which he described his experiences with this brief prayer. The book has become the classic statement of what can happen when one takes this kind of prayer seriously.

The Pilgrim met a kindly father of the church who shared with him the teaching of *The Philokalia,* a collection of the mystical and ascetical writings of Eastern Orthodox fathers over a period of eleven centuries. Primarily the father read to him about the Jesus prayer.

"Sit down alone and in silence," said the book. "Lower your head, shut your eyes, breathe out gently and imagine yourself looking into your own heart. Carry your mind, that is, your thoughts, from your head to your heart. As you breathe out, say 'Lord Jesus Christ, have mercy on me.' Say it moving your lips gently, or simply say it in your mind. Try to put all other thoughts aside. Be calm, be patient, and repeat the process very frequently."

The Pilgrim found a job as a gardener, where he could live in a little hut and say his prayer over and over.

At first his praying went very well. Then it began to tire him. He felt lazy and bored.

He returned to the father for more instruction. Again the father read from the holy book.

"If after a few attempts you do not succeed in reaching the realm of your heart in the way you have been taught, do what I am about to say, and by God's help you will find what you seek. The faculty of pronouncing words lies in the throat. Reject all other thoughts (you can do this if you will) and allow that faculty to repeat only the following words constantly, 'Lord Jesus Christ, have mercy on me.' Compel yourself to do it always. If you succeed for a time, then without a doubt your heart also will open to prayer. We know it from experience."

The father gave the Pilgrim a rosary for counting his prayers, and told him to say the prayer three thousand times a day in the beginning.

At first the Pilgrim found this burdensome; but after a few days he came to enjoy it. When he would stop, he had a desire to keep saying the prayer.

He reported again to the father.

This time the father increased his assignment to six thousand times a day.

A week later, he increased it to twelve thousand times a day.

"And that is how I go about now," wrote the Pilgrim, "and ceaselessly repeat the Prayer of Jesus, which is more precious and sweet to me than anything in the world. At times I do as much as forty-three or forty-four miles a day, and do not feel that I am walking at all. I am aware only of the fact that I am saying my

Prayer. When the bitter cold pierces me, I begin to say my Prayer more earnestly and I quickly get warm all over. When hunger begins to overcome me, I call more often on the Name of Jesus, and I forget my wish for food. When I fall ill and get rheumatism in my back and legs, I fix my thoughts on the Prayer and do not notice the pain. If anyone harms me I have only to think, 'How sweet is the Prayer of Jesus!' and the injury and the anger alike pass away and I forget it all."

It is possible of course to see a kind of neuroticism in the Pilgrim's obsession with the Jesus prayer, for he eventually came to care for nothing in the world but saying the prayer. As followers of Jesus, who went about teaching and preaching and healing, we have much more to do in the world than continually induce self-hypnosis through an incantation of Jesus' name.

But the Pilgrim's excess should in no way put us off the use of such a prayer; it is an ancient and honorable prayer, and one you will find rewarding. Try it for brief periods each day—say, ten or fifteen minutes—and see if this does not induce a sense of Christ's presence in your life.

◄《 The Use of Nonsense Syllables 》►

THE WAY THE PILGRIM used the Jesus prayer bordered on the use of the nonverbal sound or nonsense syllables as a method of achieving a near-hypnotic trance.

It suggests the possibility of using indiscriminate sounds or syllables for the same end.

This reminds us that many "authorities" who seek to instruct others in receiving the controversial gift of speaking in tongues advise the person praying to begin babbling various syllables until the Spirit takes over and leads in the speaking.

"Bub bub a loo la hum ta rah dum," the person might say.

Or "Jub a roo, jub a roo, da da cah ta too."

As a person relaxes and lets the syllables simply roll out, without any attempt to plan or control them, merely following wherever the impulse leads, he or she may enter a semi-ecstatic state in which the sounds seem to "take over," as it were, producing utterance on their own with no conscious assistance from the speaker.

This, I think, is what occurs in most tongues-speaking.

But it ought not to be too quickly dismissed, as a form of private devotion, by those who are sociologically conditioned to regard tongues-speaking as a barbaric and divisive form of religious behavior. Basically it is an attempt to break through the rational barriers that circumscribe the religious experience, allowing the subconscious part of the worshiper's being to join in the praising of God. In Freudian terms, the *Id* is released to dance and sing before God, where previously only the *Super-Ego* was permitted to speak to him. Long starved for the presence of the Holy by the forces of culture, including the organized church, it breaks forth with an emotional power that excites the person tremendously, for the person has probably felt nothing like it since the untrammeled days of childhood. It is like a personal, private Pentecost!

We remember what Thomas Kelly said, "We pray, and yet it is not we who pray, but a Greater who prays in us"; and "the autonomy of the inner life becomes complete" when we are "joyfully *prayed through* by a Seeking Life that flows through us."

Using the words of scripture or the Jesus prayer probably helps to imprint a religious "message" in the unconscious; but this complete release of the unconscious through impulses disconnected from words and meaning is probably very beneficial to some persons, especially those who have lived too strictly under the tyrannizing tendencies of their own wills and rationalities.

I have known people whose whole lives were radically changed by submission to such prayer, because the praying opened them to the abundant joy of God's presence in *all* their activities, not only in prayer. They had *heard* that God is love—had heard it with their ears and minds. But in praying like this they *experienced* him as love in their total beings.

✦℃ Praying with a Mental Image ℈✦

WHILE WE ARE on the subject of the irrational in prayer, I will mention the use of a consciously selected image as a focus for praying. This kind of prayer is also nonverbal in nature, and permits the participation of both the conscious mind and the unconscious aspects of personality.

Instead of praying with words, you select an image or scene and project yourself into that.

You might think of yourself, for example, as a piece

of wood bobbing along on the ever-moving waves of the ocean.

God is the water under you, supporting and cradling you.

With your eyes shut, you allow yourself to float with the wood, up and down, up and down.

If your imagination is especially keen, you can soon smell the clean, salt air and hear the screeing of the gulls overhead. Your body is totally relaxed, and your mind is simply drifting with the wood, letting God take care of everything.

This is an excellent technique for relaxing, and can be used as a helpful prelude to other kinds of prayer. In itself, it is also a very meaningful way of letting yourself *feel* the goodness of God in your whole being and not only in your mind.

You can of course feel *other* aspects of God's relationship to you as well.

If your praying has led you to contrition for some sinful attitude or deed, you may wish to imagine the bit of wood tossed wildly about during a fierce sea storm. Thus you are able to experience God's love (for you do not sink!) and his punishment at the same time.

The range of images for this kind of prayer is limited only by your own imagination or power to conceive them.

I have tried this way of praying in an art gallery, with astonishing effect.

Standing before the image of a blazing sun on a desert landscape, I experienced the presence of God as a withering, constant blast of heat, purging my soul with dryness and desiccation. Then, imagining the same scene in an arctic climate, I welcomed the presence as warmth and comfort against the freezing snow and ice.

Looking into the cool shadows of a great forest, I imagined myself walking there as in a cathedral of trees, a primeval sheltering, and felt the hush of all the earth, as though God hovered over it in awesome benediction.

Staring at a painting of a family—a Flemish family, I think it was—gathered in a sixteenth-century country kitchen, I became entranced by the small black kitten playing under one of the chairs. At once I imagined myself as the kitten in God's kitchen, enjoying the bowl of milk set down for me, playing among the chair legs and people's feet, and stretching languorously by the great fireplace where a kettle of soup was merrily boiling.

And so on, through dozens of pictures.

When I emerged from the gallery, I felt as if I had had a rare treat, and had experienced both the artist's works and the presence of God in a unique fashion.

✦❲ Fantasized Images ❳✦

A SLIGHT VARIATION of praying with images occurs when we make a less conscious effort to select an image and allow the image to emerge freely from the unconscious.

To do this, you must relax the mind and permit the image to float into your consciousness with the certainty that you will consider it as a prayer-image regardless of what it is.

You may be surprised.

With no threat of censorship, the image may speak of hate or violence or lust.

But let it alone if it does!

What you are after are the images from your unconscious—the things *it* bids you pray about.

Once you have got the image or images (you may wish to allow several to float up before you return to full consciousness and shut off the flow), you can pray about them. Lay them out one at a time before God and ask, "Lord, what does this image say about me? What is my subconscious mind trying to introduce into our conversation?" Then listen quietly, attentively, for the silent voice of God as he speaks to you about the image.

Another thing you can try is to let the image float into your consciousness, then allow it to do whatever it wants to, to move in any direction it wishes, even to speak, if it shows inclination to do so.

Again you may be surprised!

I have a vivid memory of praying this way once while lying on the sofa as my wife prepared dinner.

First, the image of a fat, jolly little elephant floated up. It had exaggeratedly large ears and eyes, and looked very much like the cartoon character known as "Dumbo, the Flying Elephant."

I "watched" the elephant walk happily along through the trees, feeling a strong identification with him. Somehow, I knew that *I* was the elephant.

He came to an opening in the trees and found a school carnival set up there, of precisely the type that was operated annually at my children's school.

Joyously, he trotted onto the giant Ferris wheel.

The wheel began going around.

Up and over it went, faster and faster.

Faster and faster and faster.

Suddenly the little elephant flew off through the air, backwards, and landed in the trees some distance away.

I was horrified until he landed in the trees, which led me to think his fall was thereby cushioned.

As my consciousness moved in closer to where he landed, however, I saw a crowd of people gathering around him, and I knew he was dead.

My little friend—I myself!—had been flung off the madly spinning wheel and killed.

"What does it mean!?" I asked in my prayer.

The answer was as plain as the image had been: I was going too fast and furiously on my own "spinning wheel," and if I did not slow down to a normal pace I was going to die.

That simple.

And I knew it was a valid message.

One would not wish to use such psychological images as the *only* form of praying, but it is an interesting additive to more orthodox methods. And it is especially helpful in bringing the less conscious aspects of the self before God.

❖❮ Praying Set Prayers ❯❖

FOR CENTURIES, many people have been helped in their private devotions by reading prayerfully the written prayers of others, and that practice is still valuable.

Many books of such prayers are available, ranging from *The Book of Common Prayer* and other liturgical helps to the collections of private prayer by figures like John Baillie, Lee Phillips, Samuel Miller, William Barclay, Michel Quoist, and Marjorie Holmes.

The important thing is to find prayers that are sensitive and that evoke the spirit of your own personality as you read them. Then read them quietly, meditating on the lines as you do so, until they become your own offerings to God.

A good substitute for a prayer book, if you do not have one, is a hymnal. Years ago, most hymnals did not have music printed in them, only words. This is still true in Great Britain and Europe. People are thus encouraged to see that the poetry of almost every hymn is actually a prayer, and that the songs of the divine service provide a prayerful continuity to all our worship.

Consider these great words from Isaac Watts:

> O God, our help in ages past,
>   Our hope for years to come,
> Our shelter from the stormy blast,
>   And our eternal home:
>
> Before the hills in order stood,
>   Or earth received her frame,
> From everlasting thou art God,
>   To endless years the same.
>
> A thousand ages in thy sight
>   Are like an evening gone,
> Short as the watch that ends the night
>   Before the rising sun.

Time like an everrolling stream,
    Bears all its sons away;
They fly, forgotten, as a dream
    Dies at the opening day.

O God, our help in ages past,
    Our hope for years to come,
Be thou our guard while life shall last,
    And our eternal home.

What a marvelous prayer that is! How it deepens our sense of the eternal Spirit and reminds our souls of their endless security in God!

Any decent hymnbook is full of such magnificent foci for meditation.

❦ Meditating on the Scriptures ❧

THIS IS SURELY one of the most ancient ways of entering into communion with God.

The very first psalm in the book of Psalms pictures the devout man as one who delights in the law of the Lord—the law embodied in the first five books of the Bible, the Pentateuch—and meditates on it day and night:

Blessed is the man
    who walks not in the counsel of the wicked,
nor stands in the way of sinners,
    nor sits in the seat of scoffers;
but his delight is in the law of the Lord,
    and on his law he meditates day and night.
He is like a tree
    planted by streams of water,

> that yields its fruit in its season,
> and its leaf does not wither.
> In all that he does, he prospers.

The early Christians clearly spent much time brooding over the Old Testament, letting God speak to their hearts about what had come to pass in their lives through the ministry of Jesus. Their preaching and teaching consisted primarily of references to God's promises in the Scriptures, and of recounting how those promises had been fulfilled in the death and resurrection of the Messiah.

Throughout the centuries of the Middle Ages, as Thomas Merton has reminded us, the principal method of the devotional life, for any who could read, was *meditatio scripturarum*—meditation on the Scriptures.

For Luther and Calvin and Wesley and their followers, it was the same.

Whenever in any age there has been an outpouring of spiritual passion, it has been directly traceable to an interest in the Scriptures and what God was saying to the world through them. We can scarcely expect a similar outpouring in our own time, or in our individual lives, apart from a similar interest.

The simplest way to meditate on the Scriptures, of course, is to sit down in your quiet place with the Bible before you and begin to read in a book you have chosen—say, Mark or Romans or the Psalms.

Read thoughtfully, letting the ideas and images tumble freely and fully in your mind.

Read as though listening for the One behind all of it.

If you have any difficulty understanding what you

are reading, or desire to be more enlightened about details of biblical times, you might wish to acquire a simple commentary, such as Barclay's or my own, to read along with the passages.*

It is important to read through a whole book, even though it takes several sittings, instead of skipping around and taking passages willy-nilly through the Bible. The writers had individual personalities, and the various books specific settings and themes; these do not emerge from short, random encounters.

You might want to keep a notebook handy for jotting down insights and biblical phrases you do not want to forget. That way you can pray over them not only once, but many times.

It is a good practice each day to memorize one verse or part of a verse from the passage you have read, and to use that as a prayer phrase in the manner we suggested earlier. In that way you carry your prayer and meditation time over into the activities of the rest of the day, and you insert the words deeply into your heart, so that you will never forget them.

When you have completed the reading of the day's passage, stopping at a natural breaking point, rest silently in the thought of what you have read, so that you feel the presence of God breaking through into your life.

The God whose mighty acts are recorded in the Bible will assure you of his reality in your own affairs.

I recall an occasion when my life had dropped below

* Note: Dr. Killinger's *Devotional Guides* to the gospels are published by Word Books. Each commentary, under a separate title as it is issued, contains twelve weeks' worth of daily studies, with a brief devotional prayer at the end of each study.

the spiritual poverty line. I had been quite busy for three months writing a very long book, and had permitted my daily devotional life to wane almost to nothing. We were living in a foreign country for the year, and I was very weary of dealing with all the small frustrations that can accompany the privilege of such a time, including the devaluation of the American dollar abroad. To top it off, my father called to say that my mother had become gravely ill and was in the intensive care unit of the hospital.

Feeling frustrated and helpless, I felt an impulse to reestablish my prayer life around readings from the Book of Acts.

I remember the day I did it. It was in early January, and I pulled my chair in front of the window where it would catch the warmth of the early afternoon sun.

I suppose I had read Acts a hundred times before, but it was as if I were reading it now for the first time.

Every verse or two, I would stop and pray. I felt God's power and love filling my life.

How wonderful the Book of Acts is! And how exciting to think that it told such a small part of what was happening in the early church in those days. It was almost entirely confined to the stories of Peter and Paul—the first half of the Book devoted to one and the second to the other. There was no mention of the Christian work in North Africa, where it was undoubtedly going on. No mention of the mission to India, where legend says Thomas went with the gospel, and where strong centers of Christian belief were later found. No mention of the work in Gaul, modern-day France, or Spain, where the Roman culture is bound to have assured a ready entrance for the apostles of Christ. Antioch, the

third-ranked city of the Roman Empire, where the followers were first called Christians in derision, received
a bare mention, no more.

What a tremendous ferment the Spirit of God was
causing in the world!

I prayed for my mother with a new heart. It was as
if I were right there in her room, four thousand miles
away.

I felt God's power anew—in my life, in hers, in the
world.

How silly we are to let a single day go by without
reading the Word and meditating on it!

❖❘❘ Fantasizing with the Scriptures ❘❘❖

WAYNE PIPKIN, in his sensitive book *Christian Meditation:
Its Art and Practice* (New York: Hawthorn Books, 1977),
suggests using the stories and teachings of Scripture as
the basis for group exercises in meditating and reflecting
on the Christian faith. I have tried this, and find that
it works equally well for both groups and individuals.

The idea is this.

First you read a passage of Scripture.

Then, to meditate on it, you close your eyes and imagine that you are entering the scene you have read about
or, if it is a passage of doctrine, that you are having a
conversation with the author about what he has said.
You give your imagination free rein for several minutes,
so that a living drama takes place in your mind.

When the meditation is over, you think about what
happened in it, what was said, and how it all applies

to your life now. You offer the insights to God and pray for faithfulness to incorporate them into your daily routines.

Here, taken from Dr. Pipkin's book, is an example of fantasized meditation. It is intended to follow a reading of 1 Corinthians 13, Paul's famous chapter on love (and also 1 Corinthians 1–12 and Acts 18:1–18, if the reader is ambitious).

In your mind's eye you are standing on the top of a hill which overlooks a city down below you. Off in the distance you can see the outline of the harbor at which there are many Roman ships. The road beneath you is paved and reaches down toward the city. Begin making your way now down the road, noticing that there are many people coming and going.

The time of day is dusk. Evening is coming fast as you continue on your way. You are coming closer to the edge of town. As you approach the first few houses on the outskirts, notice that there is a path which goes off to the side and takes you away from the main thoroughfare. As you continue down this path, observe that it brings you to a small cottage which is set aside from the rest. Approach the entrance of the cottage slowly, in anticipation of your visit.

As you come to the doorway of the cottage, notice that the evening has come in its entirety and that there is a warm glow emanating from the windows and the door. As you stand for a moment at the door, looking into the cottage, notice that there is a man sitting inside. He is writing.

As you stand for a moment, he notices your presence and stops his writing and stands and comes to greet you. It is Paul and he has been expecting you. He invites you into the cottage. As you enter, be aware of the colors in the room and of the meager yet comfortable furnishings. Paul invites you to sit down facing him.

After the initial greetings, he mentions that he has just

finished writing a hymn on love which he is including in the letter he is writing to his friends at Corinth.

Now you will have some time to visit with Paul, to talk with him about the Hymn to Love. Feel free to say what is on your mind and to wait for Paul also to speak his mind to you. This time is yours for that conversation.

(Pause four minutes)

Now it is time for your conversation with Paul to draw to a close. Knowing that you can return anytime you wish, make your way to the door of the cottage and say your farewells to Paul. After looking one last time about the room where you have been engaged in conversation, make your exit and start back up the path toward the outskirts of town.

As you make your way up the path, do not try to think on the meaning of the conversation you have just had. There is plenty of time for that later. Just be aware of the feelings that you have after having had the conversation.

Feel free as you make your way back to the top of the path to begin to come back into the normal state of consciousness at your own pace. Do not hurry, but come back at a relaxed pace, at whatever pace is comfortable for you.

Welcome back (pp. 87–88).

Try this meditation experience yourself. Read it again, as far as the pause. Then close your eyes and imagine your own visit with Paul. When a few minutes have elapsed, make your way back to consciousness.

A "debriefing" is supposed to follow the meditation when it is used with a group. This consists of sharing aloud the mental images people received of the place where they were—the town, the house, the furnishings, the appearance of Paul—and finally the special insights that came as a result of the "visit."

You can debrief yourself if you use the meditation privately, and then ponder the insights in prayer.

If you are imaginative, the practice can yield marvelous results.

I used this particular meditation once with a group of ministers and seminarians. Afterwards, in the debriefing, one minister told us he had some difficulty getting into the meditation because he was dreading a meeting he had that evening with a terrible woman in his parish who was on the warpath against him. Finally, though, he got into it enough to ask Paul what he should do about the woman.

Paul's reply: "Love her."

The minister thought about that all the way home, he told us later.

That night, he went into the meeting with a new feeling about the woman.

"You know," he said, "she was different. Or *I* was different. I don't know which it was, but we got along beautifully. Our relationship was improved enormously!"

The thirteenth chapter of 1 Corinthians had become really personalized for him.

❧ Meditating on Other Literature ☙

WE ARE NOT CONFINED to meditating on Scripture, of course. There are many kinds of literature that offer insights and impressions well worth reflecting on and praying about.

Almost any bookstore offers a shelf full of books with devotional readings and meditation pieces.

There are several little magazines that feature material to be used in this fashion; *Guideposts, Open Windows, Alive Now!,* and *The Upper Room* are but four of them.

And then there are all the "secular" books.

Books of poetry can dazzle us with images that become springboards to prayer. The poems of Robert Frost. And T. S. Eliot. And Robert Lowell. And Gerard Manley Hopkins.

They may even prompt you to write little poems of your own, which become prayer offerings to God.

And there are the beautiful, sensitive writings of such persons as Annie Dillard, Frederick Buechner, May Sarton, Madeleine L'Engle, Mary C. Richards, Nikos Kazantzakis, James Herriott, and Elie Wiesel.

I literally prayed my way through Dillard's *Pilgrim at Tinker Creek* and Buechner's *Alphabet of Grace*, they are so profound and so exquisitely written.

And Kazantzakis, with his Greek Orthodox ebullience, always makes me feel so much more alive to the resurrection of Christ and its effect on the world—especially in *Zorba the Greek.*

Some people, I know, are afraid of literature that is not specifically "Christian."

That is most unfortunate.

No walls of orthodoxy or chains of tradition were able to bind our Lord. He went everywhere, touching the unclean as well as the clean, eating with sinners as well as Pharisees.

And, if the Gospels are any kind of record, he enjoyed the sinners more than the Pharisees.

But this is a matter you must decide for yourself.

✦⟨ Giving Thanks for All Things ⟩✦

"Praise the lord!" sang the psalmist. "O give thanks to the Lord, for he is good; for his steadfast love endures for ever!" (Psalms 106:1).

Thanksgiving has always been one of the most delightful forms of prayer.

Do you remember the story of Jesus and the ten lepers (Luke 17:11–19)? The lepers came asking to be healed. Jesus told them to go and show themselves to the priests in the temple. It was to be an act of faith on their part, for the law in Leviticus 13 and 14 provided that anyone who had been cleansed of leprosy must present himself to the priests for certification of cleanliness before being restored to society. On the way, they were all healed. In their excitement, they all ran on their way to the temple and their families.

All but one, that is.

One remembered, and came back to thank the Lord.

"Where are the others?" asked Jesus. "Were all of them too busy to return and praise God except this foreigner?" (my paraphrase).

There was the poignancy of the story. A *foreigner.*

A "nonreligious" person.

All the rest were too busy.

Jesus blessed the foreigner and sent him happily on his way.

That is something we often miss—the blessing of the thanksgiving.

If we do not take time to meditate on the countless

gifts of God, and to thank him for them, we lose many wonderful moments that would even further enrich our lives.

Sometimes, because we are not thankful, we become sorry for ourselves, and feel neglected.

It is in being thankful that we see how truly rich we are.

I have a friend who works with the deaf. Her work is very demanding and exhausting. Some days she begins to feel tired and depressed.

But she is a woman of prayer.

"Whenever I begin to feel depressed," she told me, "I think of something for which I am happy, and I say 'Thank you, Lord.' Then I think of something else for which I am happy. Again I say 'Thank you, Lord.' Then I think of something else, and say it again.

"Before I know it, I've completely forgotten about being depressed, and my whole day is bright again!"

That is a wonderful testimony.

I was speaking at a conference in North Carolina, and told of her experience.

The next day at breakfast a woman came up to me.

"I have something to tell you," she said. "Do you remember sharing with us the story of the woman who gave thanks? Well, this morning about three o'clock my husband woke up with a terrible pain. He had gone swimming in a motel pool when we were on our way to the conference, and developed an inner ear infection. It had gotten much worse during the night. When he woke up, the room was going round and round for him, and he was in awful agony.

"I didn't know what to do. I went out into the hall of our dormitory and knocked on a door. I told the man who came to the door that I needed help, and he got dressed and drove us to the emergency room of the hospital.

"An intern looked in my husband's ears but said he didn't know very much about such problems. He gave him some medicine and told us to come back at seven, when another doctor would be there.

"The medicine didn't help. We came back to our room and my husband was screaming with pain.

"Then we thought of your friend and the thanksgiving. We were on the bed. I was sitting on the edge and was holding my husband's head in my arms, trying to comfort him. I thought of something in my life I was thankful for and gave thanks for it. My husband, in his pain, did the same. I thought of something else. So did he.

"That was what we did until seven o'clock," she said. "We gave thanks for the blessings in our lives. I thought you would want to know how much it helped."

At seven they had returned to the hospital and the doctor had given him an antibiotic and a sedative. He was resting comfortably when she came to the cafeteria to get some breakfast.

Try it yourself.

Not just when you're in distress, but as a daily method of prayer.

Most of us have no idea how rich we are.

Simply listen, in your time of silence, to the voice of the Spirit suggesting things for which you should give thanks.

Then, each time, say a quiet thank you.

I think you will understand better than ever before the Mystery of God's loving care.

✦❰ Blessing Your Memories ❱✦

A SIMILAR WAY of praying is by blessing your memories.

The idea is to evoke your memories one by one, holding them before God for a few moments and thanking him for them as you do.

Painful memories as well as pleasant ones. They too are part of the fabric of your existence. They help to make you what you are today. And, if God accepts you as you are, then you can accept your memories as they are.

Actually this is a kind of therapy, for it is a positive way of dealing with parts of your past you have never been able to fully accept.

Let's suppose you are a man in your middle years. You are in your second marriage; your first wife left you after only two years of marriage. You have three children, aged twelve to twenty. Your middle child, who is fifteen, had rheumatic fever and has never been able to play normally at sports or do anything that required much energy. You do not consider yourself a success in business, for you have changed careers twice and are now an insurance underwriter whose monthly pay will not quite meet all the bills; your wife must work half time as a store clerk to help out. Your father, with whom you never got along, died when you were married to your first wife. Your mother is a partial invalid living with your only sister, and your sister complains about your not shouldering more of the load by keeping your mother part of the time. Your health is not as good as it was, and you are beginning to be troubled by frequent pains of arthritis in your hips and back.

How do you bless your memories?

Begin by recalling some *good* memories.

Perhaps the time you went fishing with your father, and he showed you how to bait your hook just right and then draw the line through the water so that the fish would leap at it.

And the time the family went out in the station wagon and cut down your own Christmas tree on the farm of someone your father knew.

And the little puppy that followed you home from the store one day and your parents said you could keep.

Lift these up to God with thanksgiving.

Then, as the memories come, don't shun the bad ones, the ones that make you wince.

Like the time you knocked the paintbrush into the dirt when your father was painting the front porch, and he walloped the daylights out of you. You hated him for that. Remember how you stalked off to the field down on the corner and hid in a clump of trees till after dark, thinking you would make him sorry? And then, when you finally did come home, he had gone off to a lodge meeting and never said a word to you about it?

Why should the memory be painful now? Oh, the event was bad enough at the time. But that was a long time ago.

Wouldn't you love to see that old porch now?

And see your father?

Try to thank God for this memory too, just as you did for the good ones.

It was heartbreaking when your little boy had the

fever and nearly died. That was an awful time. You didn't sleep for nights on end. Not until he was out of danger and you couldn't stay awake any more.

But think about how close you've been to that boy ever since. Maybe, if he had been able to lead a normal life, you wouldn't have had so much fellowship with him. There's nothing like an affliction in a child to create a bond between him and his parents.

Can you remember that illness now and give thanks for God's presence in it and all the events that followed?

Your first wife really hurt you when she walked off, didn't she? Hurt your pride. Left you alone. Life seemed to be over for a while there, didn't it?

You don't like to think about it now.

But do think about it.

Think how it was part of her growing up, and part of yours.

Think how you would never have married your present wife if it hadn't happened as it did, or had the children you have.

You can forgive her now, can't you?

And thank God for that memory, too?

Try this kind of praying sometime when you are in a reminiscent mood. It is an immensely rich form of prayer, for it brings to vivid presence the many experiences through which you have already lived.

It also has a theological validity.

The history of the faith of Israel, as we know it in the Bible, is primarily a *recounting* of the events in the life of the people, and a meditation on how God has been involved in those events.

When you sit prayerfully recalling the events in *your* life, both large and small, and then bless them by giving thanks to God for having lived the events and being able to remember them, you are engaging in the same kind of theological act.

It will deepen your faith by letting you see the panorama of years under the loving care of the heavenly Father. The result will be a greater steadiness in future times of crisis and pain.

"This too shall pass," you will think, "and become part of the history of my life. It is good to live, and to give thanks to God!"

❖❰ Praying About Your Work ❱❖

THE AVERAGE YOUNG PERSON or adult spends at least half of his or her time in some form of work or serious activity.

It is only fitting that this should become the subject of our prayers.

Not in order to "succeed" in the world's eyes, or to make more money, but to be fulfilled.

To be creative in our use of the talents and gifts God has given us.

To be thoughtful of others in the way we do our work.

One of Jesus' most important parables (Matthew 25:14–30, Luke 19:12–27) was about three men entrusted with money to invest for their master. Two were energetic, creative fellows and earned their master's hearty approval. The third was slothful and dull, and was discharged by the master.

The parable was actually about the Pharisees, who had been unimaginative stewards of God's grace.

But Jesus clearly had respect for careful, eager workmen; otherwise the point of the parable would not have been so well made.

God *is* concerned about our work, as he is concerned about the other aspects of our lives, and this should encourage us to bring our work before him when we pray.

Prayer relates our subconscious lives to our conscious lives. To brood about our work in prayer enables the Spirit to release hidden power and insight from the subconscious levels of our being, so that they may be used in doing our work.

If you are an athlete, prayer will help you tap the deeper levels of your prowess and energy as an athlete.

If you are a physicist, prayer will encourage you to take those intuitive leaps of the mind that Einstein and others have said are so indispensable to scientific progress.

If you are an artist, prayer will help you to overcome the gap between the creative impulse and the artistic performance, so that currents of inspiration flow through your mind and hands with less resistance.

If you are a housewife, prayer will bring you to a more thoughtful, resourceful attitude toward the repetitive tasks of your vocation such as cleaning, cooking, and decorating.

The idea is to concentrate in your prayer upon what it is you have to do, either as an immediate job or as a lifelong vocation.

Thank God for your work, which is actually one of the greatest blessings of your life.

Then wait patiently in the silence and listen. Let the Spirit speak to your heart about new ways of approaching what you do.

About how to make the best use of your energy.

About what parts of your work may be unnecessary expenditures of your time and power.

Paul Tournier, the Swiss physician, said that one of the most important aspects of his prayer has always been to have God tell him what he should *not* undertake to do. Praying in that way has helped him keep his schedule simpler and more manageable, and has doubtless prolonged his life, for there are many calls upon his time.

David prayed about the temple he wanted to build for God, said Dr. Tournier, and God told him not to build it. If David had disregarded that and built the temple, it would have been a sin, even though David would have been doing it for God.

In the same way today, God will tell us not to do certain things that in themselves seem very praiseworthy.

He helps us to shape our work and our lives so that they are fulfilled in him.

Then, like Brother Lawrence, the famous lay brother of the Carmelites in the seventeenth century, we will feel that we are worshiping him as well when we are scrubbing the pots and pans as we can worship him at High Mass in the cathedral!

❖€ Praying About Your Dreams ❀

WE HAVE SPOKEN often of prayer and the unconscious.

Nowhere does the relationship grow stronger than when we learn to pray about our dreams.

Dreams have always had an enormous significance in biblical faith.

In the stories of Joseph and the Pharaoh (Genesis 40–41).

Of Nebuchadnezzar and Daniel (Daniel 2–4).

Of Joseph and the angel of the Lord (Matthew 1:20–21).

Of the Magi and the warning not to return to Herod (Matthew 2:12).

Of Joseph and the warning to flee into Egypt (Matthew 2:13), and then to return to Israel (Matthew 2:19–20).

Of Pilate's wife, who "suffered much" over Jesus in a dream (Matthew 27:19).

Of innumerable "visions," many of which were probably dreams.

Many people through the ages have respected dreams as having not only reality, but *super*reality. That is, they predict the future. They show things that are happening presently in other locales.

Whatever we believe about that, there can be no doubt in our minds today that dreams tell a great deal about the unconscious life of the person dreaming them. Psychological research has taught us much about this, and is revealing more all the time.

When we sleep, the unconscious is freed from the repression mechanisms that are ordinarily at work in our minds. It is no longer subject to the rules of daytime "reality," and can run riot into the wild provinces of absurdity that are a part of our larger reality.

To the psychiatrist, dreams and parts of dreams that are remembered when we awaken are invaluable clues to the inner personality, to the part of us that is often beaten and abused and stuffed into a box by our conscious minds.

Research has shown that most of us have several dreams each night, even though we may think when we awaken that we have slept without any dreams at all. We tend to remember only those dreams or parts of dreams that coincide with a waking moment—a time when a gas pain struck or a bed-partner made us turn over or a sharp noise interrupted our sleep.

It is possible to train yourself to be more conscious of your dreams, paradoxical as that may sound. Some persons actually set alarm clocks to wake them at various hours of the night, so that they will be able to catch the dreams that occur at those times. Then they write down the content they can remember from those dreams and go back to sleep. Eventually they become more sensitive to the dreaming process, and are able to awaken automatically when having a dream.

What do dreams mean? Since ancient times, men and women have tried to discover their significance.

"We have had dreams," said the Pharaoh's officers to Joseph, "and there is no one to interpret them."

Joseph answered: "Do not interpretations belong to God?" (Genesis 40:8).

Do they not indeed? A psychiatrist may understand

a great deal about dreams. But the Spirit of God is supremely able to help us in the process of understanding our inner selves in terms of the images that come to us in our sleep, and to put that in the perspective of God's will for our lives.

The significance of this for prayer and the self is remarkable. Whenever we can come before God with a dream or part of a dream and say "Lord, here is what I have dreamed, how is it important to my life?" we have a greater chance of discovering what it is like to be whole in the Kingdom of God.

Let me give an example.

Recently, while living in Oxford, I had a dream in which I met a young woman. Her hair was tangled and unclean, and she was wearing, among other things, a pair of extremely tattered old slacks; there were great rips in them. I was on my way home and she attached herself to me and followed me there. On the way, we went through a sort of alleyway, a public thoroughfare, and it was rather crowded. Among the people we passed there was a woman I had known for many years. A somewhat uppity person, she stared in disdain at the woman who was so unkempt and disheveled, and at me for being in her company.

The poor woman and I passed into the house, which was an elegant place with potted ferns, a marble fireplace, and expensive furniture—the sort of house one sees in television programs set in well-to-do Victorian homes. It was nothing like the various homes I have lived in.

Inside, she followed me around, chattering about this and that. I remember two things distinctly. One, she was very free to reach out and touch me, something that shocked me a bit in view of her station in life. And, two, once she spoke a rather rapid sentence to me in German, which I did not understand. This, of course, puzzled me, as she did not appear to be a person of much education.

At the end of this scenario, I drifted into semi-consciousness, and fastened upon what I then took to be the salient features of the dream, determined upon remembering them when I woke up. Those features were, in order, the woman in tattered slacks, the haughty woman who saw us coming to my house, the first woman's freedom to touch me, and her speaking to me in German.

I was also conscious of praying, at the time, to know the meaning of the dream, and of understanding instantly why the woman was in tattered slacks.

For months, on the streets of Oxford, I had seen a woman, about fifty, I would say, who was almost invariably wearing the same faded and torn pair of slacks. She looked very poor; but she appeared, instead of having been poor all her life, to have fallen on hard times.

Usually I had seen her at a distance and she was walking rather briskly, as if she had a determinate goal, so that, though I had often had the impulse to approach her and offer her some financial help, I had not done so. Then, about two weeks before the dream, I had seen her in the grocery store where I was shopping. When I came out of the store, she was standing outside, apparently engaged in serious thought about something; I surmised that she was calculating whether she could afford something she had seen in the store. Determined to press five or ten pounds upon her, I stepped up to speak to her. But in the instant I did she bolted away like an animal that has been frightened. Fearful of offending her, I did not follow, but got into my car, which was parked nearby, and started home. A block or so further along, I saw her again, walking very slowly along an open space on the sidewalk, apparently pondering something again. Pulling the car over to the curb and rolling down the window, I attempted to speak to her again. But once more she rushed away as if she had not heard me. I drove home feeling very badly, for I wanted to help her in whatever distress she was suffering. I was afraid I had been too timid in approaching her, and should have acted more boldly.

I knew when I prayed that the dream was at least partly about her, and I felt that God was saying to me that I must make a stronger effort to give her aid.

As I awakened the next morning, I awakened into prayer, as my custom is, and found the dream very much the center of the prayer. Why was the haughty woman in the dream? I asked God. Though I had known her for years, it had also been years since I had seen her, and we were never very close. Was she in some kind of trouble? I wondered, and prayed for her.

The young woman in the dream did not look like the middle-aged woman I had seen on the streets of Oxford; in fact, she resembled a young woman I had seen in a recent BBC production of Thomas Hardy's *The Mayor of Casterbridge*. And her speech and manners were more like those of a Puerto Rican girl I had seen interviewed on a program featuring a high school in New York's Harlem section. Was that why she touched me so freely?

And what about her use of German, which seemed totally incongruent with her other speech and level of education? As I meditated on the dream in my prayer time later in the day, I remembered that I was soon scheduled to make a trip to Germany to speak to American troops and their wives there. Perhaps that was related. I prayed for my usefulness on that trip.

In yet another prayer time, I thought of the expensive home to which I had repaired with the poor young woman. It was obviously very luxurious. This led me to pray that I might be more successful in sharing my possessions with others less fortunate than I and my family.

Sometime later, reflecting on the dream once more, it occurred to me that the presence of the young woman and her touching me reminded me of my younger sister, who had been killed in an accident when we were both children. I didn't know why this was, for the girl in no way resembled my sister. But I prayed for my sister and gave thanks to God for the privilege of knowing her even for a few years.

I hope I have not bored you by recounting all of this, but I did want you to see how thoroughly useful dreams can be for helping us to reflect on our lives before God because they come from the other side of consciousness.

My own practice is to go to sleep praying, whether I am taking a nap or lying down for the night, and to awaken in the same manner. That way, I feel that I am entrusting the night and its "messages" to God in such a way that the messages, however pleasant or unpleasant, become constructively related to my waking hours. Even a nightmare, which I am thankful to say I rarely have, can offer useful provender for the ongoing life of prayer.

◄ Praying for Other Persons ►

IN THE PRECEDING CHAPTER I mentioned praying for the haughty woman who appeared in one of my dreams. I know several people deeply grounded in prayer who are very careful to pray for the persons who occur to them in dreams or other forms of random thought. They sometimes refer to thoughts about other persons as "impulses," and feel that there is often a good reason, even a supernatural one, that has led them to remember a particular person at a particular moment.

I have spoken in *Bread for the Wilderness, Wine for the Journey* (Waco, Tex.: Word Books, 1976) of one woman who seems to have uncanny powers of perception in this regard. Several times I have had a letter from her saying that she knew I was passing through some crisis of decision or time of illness, and was praying for me. Each time she has been correct. She also writes to another friend in the same manner, and has not erred in his case either.

This woman follows a very traditional and useful method of keeping a prayer list with the names of many persons on it. She reviews it each time she prays, interceding briefly for each person named on the list. But she also waits for God's Spirit over the list, so that the impulses she feels are often, I think, divinely given. Then, when she feels an impulse, she prays with real concentration for the person thus singled out.

The trouble with a prayer list, said C. S. Lewis, is that, given a few years, it can become so burdensomely *long*. Yet he could never bring himself to lop off any names from it. He would intend to; it seemed so absolutely necessary. But then, each time he would go to do it, he would say, "No, not today. Another time, perhaps."

We can understand his feeling. It is almost like deciding not to bring someone before God any more, without knowing whether or not the person will get there on his own!

It is probably best to make a *written* prayer list.

I have never done so. I try to keep a *mental* list, and sometimes I will be reminded of someone for whom I have forgotten to pray for a while and will feel very much ashamed of myself.

I do often in my prayers allow my mind to roam over the entire country, from East to West and from North to South, remembering people I know in all the states, and then think of the ones I know in other parts of the world.

But I really *ought* to keep a written list.

And of course we should pray for people we don't know, as well as the ones we do.

The world is so full of hunger and poverty and suffering of many varieties, including even the suffering of those who have too much of the world's goods instead of too little.

It is all right to pray for the poor or the hungry of whole nations *en bloc*, I suppose; there is hardly a way of avoiding it. But I also favor narrowing down the object of prayer as much as possible, and beseeching God for such subgroups and individuals as all the men in Karachi over sixty or all the women going through childbirth in Soweto or all the six-year-olds going to bed hungry in Calcutta. Somehow this seems a little more personal and even more manageable.

It is easy enough when you begin to pray for others (and sometimes even after years of such praying) to wonder what good it can possibly do the persons you are praying for.

This is not the place to deal with that problem. I have tried to treat it in *Bread for the Wilderness, Wine for the Journey.* But Christians have always believed that it does make a difference when you pray for someone. Not just in you and your attitude, but in the possibilities for the other person.

Think of it this way: In a world where energy is the true basis for all life, prayer effects a transmission of your energy through the medium of God's Spirit to the person in need of that energy, regardless of how far away from you he or she may be.

It is not that you are trying to countermand God's will for the person. Indeed, you pray *within* God's will and ask that it be done.

But you are lending your willful energy to God for that person's use if God wills that the person have it.

Beyond that, you need not question. Your part is merely to lend your energy. And if you have been faithful in your devotional life, so that your faith in God is firmly grounded, you will then be able to accept with gratitude whatever he wills for the person.

Some persons pray for others by merely thinking or mentioning aloud their names together with whatever it is they feel should be asked for the persons.

Others say they like instead to concentrate on the faces of those they are praying for, getting a mental picture and simply holding it for a little while there in the presence of God.

I personally favor doing both.

First I wait quietly, thinking about the person until I get a clear image.

I try to listen to the Spirit, to see if I can hear what it is the person really needs.

Then I make an actual petition for the person, always concluding with something like the phrase, "Your will be done," for it would be most arrogant to assume that I was invariably right about what he or she requires.

Having used the word *energy* as a metaphor for what happens in intercessory prayer, I should say a brief word here about prayers for the dead.

Our Roman Catholic friends have always believed that it is a duty to continue to pray for the souls of those who have died, and also that those who have died can continue to pray for us.

Although the Bible does not make much of this idea, it does speak of baptism for the dead (1 Corinthians 15:29), and seems to support praying for them in at least a couple of ways. One is in Jesus' story of the rich man and Lazarus (Luke 16:19–31), in which the rich man who has died and is in torment carries on a dialogue with God, first about his own suffering and then about warning his brothers who have not yet died. Another is the imagery throughout the book of Revelation, which seems to suggest a kind of universal complicity in prayer and yearning that involves both the saints still living on earth and those living in heaven.

I think it is a good idea for us to accept the notion much as the New Testament does, without either setting it at the center of our belief and concerns or dismissing it entirely, but, when we feel the inclination, to remember in prayer those who have died and to take comfort in believing that they also pray for us.

On this point, I rather like what C. S. Lewis said to his friend Malcolm Muggeridge: "At our age the majority of those we love best are dead. What sort of intercourse with God could I have if what I love best were unmentionable to Him?"

Again, I believe the word *energy* may be the key.

The first law of energy is that it can be neither created nor destroyed. It can only be moved around.

What becomes of the energy of the soul of one who dies? I believe it still exists for us—if indeed it was ever *for* us before the death. And I see little reason that the transference of energy through prayer that occurred during life should stop because a person's body has died.

But I do not wish to persuade you of something that is against the grain of your natural inclination for belief. It is a matter you must decide for yourself. And there are certainly enough persons for you to worry about among the living without troubling yourself too much about the dead!

The important thing is for you to learn in prayer to make your own energies available to God in behalf of other persons who need them. Intercessory prayer is indispensable, regardless of what other kind of prayer we normally prefer.

In no other way, I think, do we realize quite so perfectly the meaning of the phrase "the communion of saints."

◀❮ Fantasized Scenes ❯▶

THIS KIND OF PRAYER is closely related to praying about one's dreams, because it involves praying about day-dreams.

It is especially useful, I find, when I am tired, depressed, or confused, and other kinds of praying seem to require more of me than I feel like giving.

In fact, it can be utterly refreshing.

The idea is to get very relaxed, imagine a scene, then let yourself "enter" the scene and wander about in it, doing whatever your unfettered self wants to do.

Afterwards, you reflect on what happened in the fantasy and offer yourself in prayer to God.

The relaxation is very, very important.

It should be done with the kind of thoroughness used by psychologists preparing people for biofeedback exercises.

You should feel it in your hands and feet, your arms and thighs, your neck and back, your chest.

Then, when you have gotten the knots out of your system and are sitting comfortably in a chair or lying comfortably on the floor or on a bed, let yourself go.

Imagine a meadow scene.

Or a seashore.

Or a lonely mountainside in the sunset.

Walk into the picture.

Enjoy it; don't hurry.

Maybe you see someone coming toward you.

Who is it?

What happens when you meet?

Perhaps you go further, either alone or with the other person.

You get the idea.

Then, when it is over and you have "come back" to yourself, to the present realities of the room where you are, meditate on the memory of what took place. Talk to God about it.

Try it. You may be surprised what you learn, and how good it feels.

Wayne Pipkin introduced me to this method after finding it in St. Ignatius.

Wayne tells about an experience he had with it. It was during a very tense time in his life. He had recently moved from the university where he was a church history professor and had become a director in a seminary system. Now the seminary was considering the possibility of closing, and it would mean that he would have no job.

He worried about how he would take care of his lovely wife and two little daughters. Perhaps they would have to sell their home and move in with one set of parents until things improved.

In the midst of this anxiety, Wayne tried this method of meditative prayer.

He imagined that he was standing on a sandy bluff overlooking the ocean. It was a beautiful, clear day, and he could feel the spray from the salt air and the wonderful odor of the sea. Seagulls were flying overhead.

He descended the bluff and walked along the shore, feeling very relaxed and at peace with the world.

As he walked, he saw a bottle floating in the waves. It appeared to have a message inside.

He watched as the bottle bobbed in the waves, constantly disappearing and reappearing, gradually washing in to shore.

Suddenly he realized that the message must be for him! Eagerly, he ran forward into the water to rescue it. Surely it was the answer to all his problems!

He caught the bottle and opened it. He removed the message, and found it was in Latin.

"Hodie Christus natus est," it said.

"Today, Christ is born."

I am sure he must have been a bit disappointed in the message at first. Puzzled, at least.

What did that have to do with anything?

But as he meditated on the saying Wayne began to see how important it was to him.

It was what he had forgotten.

"Today, Christ is born."

The central fact of Christianity was more important than his problems and anxieties. Slowly, surely, it moved back to the center of his consciousness, displacing all his worries.

"I had become so obsessed with the future," said Wayne, "that I had forgotten the central affirmation which gave meaning and hope for the present. When the words appeared to me on the page in the context of that meditation, it was not an idle affirmation of faith. Rather, it was a rekindling of faith down at the very roots of my being. In the midst of apparent insecurity, I discovered an insight into lasting security."

It was a thrilling discovery!

May I relate a similar experience of my own?

It was in the month of March. I was extremely tired. I had spent all of January wrestling with a vocational decision. Then in February my wife's mother had an operation and died, and we made several trips home. My Lenten speaking schedule had gotten out of hand, and I seemed to be running off in all directions when I was not in class with my students. My emotional tension seemed to be about a hundred percent higher than I could stand, and going higher all the time.

One day I lay on the bed and fell asleep.

As I was coming out of the sleep into semi-consciousness, I began a fantasy meditation.

I imagined that I was walking out the curving driveway to the mailbox in front of our house.

It was a warm, beautiful spring day, and the birds were singing.

Flowers were blooming all over the yard—daffodils, tulips, and crocuses.

The dogwoods were blooming too.

When I reached the mailbox and opened it, there was a letter there.

I knew it was the message I needed, just as Wayne had known when he saw the bottle.

I could hardly wait to open it!

My fingers fumbled at it nervously.

At last I had it out.

It said, "God is love."

That was all.

"God is love."

It was exactly what I needed to hear.

Down beneath it all—the vocational struggle, the death of a loved one, the physical exhaustion and the tension—was the unshakable love of God.

Tears filled my eyes as I lay there on the bed, and I gulped, "Thank you."

I felt completely refreshed when I got up.
It was just what I needed!
Try it yourself sometime.
It may be what you need too.

❧ An Imaginary Conversation with Christ ☙

WALTER SAVAGE LANDER, a nineteenth-century literary
figure, wrote a famous series of *Imaginary Conversations*
that depicted great persons of history talking with each
other. Some of the insights provoked by these conversations are amazing.

Suppose you were to carry on a similar conversation
with Christ. What do you think it might reveal?

The secret of such a conversation is to write it in
the form of a dramatic dialogue, and to do so without
pausing to think while writing. That is, the flow of dialogue should be as spontaneous as possible, with the
unconscious side of your being supplying most of the
words.

Here is how a sample dialogue might look:

ME: Lord, I am feeling totally self-satisfied these days.
Does that mean I have been out of touch with you?

CHRIST: Maybe you have been out of touch with my
little ones who are suffering.

ME: You mean the poor? I know I am well off.

CHRIST: I have many little ones who are starving to death—in Asia, in Africa, in Latin America.

ME: But they are so far away. What can I do about them?

CHRIST: What have you tried to do?

ME: Well . . . nothing, I suppose. I do give at church.

CHRIST: What do you give—a few dollars? What is that compared to the enormous suffering of my little ones? If they were your children, you would do anything to save them. *Anything.*

I confess that this is one of my own imaginary dialogues. It was a scathing one, and led to my making a greater effort to serve Christ through the hungry of the world.

Not all the dialogues are as self-indicting as this one. Often they are strengthening or comforting. And sometimes they are filled with love and peace and the simple joy of relationship.

The words in such conversations can hardly be taken as the real words of Jesus to us. But it is entirely possible that the Spirit of Christ does release understandings from deep within us that convey striking insights we could not attain by ourselves.

And the important thing, once we have discovered the insights, is to focus on them in prayer and meditation until we feel our lives submitting to God's presence. Then we know that the imaginary dialogue has led to real togetherness!

❧ Subconscious Writing ❧

THIS METHOD OF PRAYING or finding insights for prayer is similar to the imaginary conversation method. Only, instead of writing a dialogue, you write simple statements as they occur to you.

Again, the important thing is not to edit anything, but to let the writing simply flow out of the inner self. Don't think of a particular sentence, "Oh, how silly! I mustn't put that down." In fact, don't think at all while you are writing. Merely get a starting sentence and begin writing.

Keep your mind loose.

Let the words tumble out without being conscious of them.

You may wish to focus your writing around a particular problem you are having or an idea that has been haunting you. You can do this by having the idea or problem in mind as you write the first sentence.

But don't exercise any more control than this. Let your subconscious mind take over.

Suppose, for example, that you were concerned about a vocational opportunity that had come your way, and wished to get some of your unconscious feelings out in the open to be considered in prayer. Your subconscious writing might read like this:

I am really concerned about that job. It has great appeal for me. I like the people I would be working with. They are very attractive. I am not valued where I am. It is terrible to work where you don't feel wanted. My parents never acted as if they wanted me. I wonder if I act as if I don't want my children. I would hate to die now, without showing them more love. If I take that job and feel more love in it, maybe I will show more love. Does God love me? I am unlovable sometimes. Maybe I would feel that way anywhere. Perhaps people love me where I am and I cannot feel it. I must sort this out.

This is an actual paragraph written by a woman in early midlife. It was her first experience with automatic writing. She was greatly surprised, examining it later, to see how much it revealed about her.

She saw that her real problem was not with her present job but with her own feelings of unworthiness. These feelings, she realized, caused her to withdraw from others. This, in turn, made her feel neglected and disliked.

As the woman focused on this insight in prayer, she came to feel more self-worth through God's acceptance of her, and decided to stay in the job where she was. She developed two goals for her life. One was to learn to interact more healthily with her colleagues at work, and the other was to show more affection toward her children.

You may find, if you like to write down your feelings, that this is a meaningful way to know your inner self better.

Begin by writing as I have suggested. Do not think about what you are writing. Concentrate instead on the *flow*.

Review what you have written, noticing any thoughts that particularly strike you.

Then meditate and pray about these, asking God to

reveal to you new understandings or new directions for your life.

And be prepared for some changes!

❧ Keeping a Prayer Journal ❧

HAVE YOU EVER kept a diary?

A prayer journal is a kind of diary, with a difference. All you enter in it are remarks about your prayer life.

The experiences you have, like the ones I recorded above.

The thoughts that come to you while you're praying.

How your prayer life is affecting the rest of your life.

What you're having trouble with in your praying.

Who you have thought of during your times of prayer.

What God seems to be asking of you as you pray.

All sorts of things like that.

It needn't be terribly formal. In fact, the more casual the better.

You can abbreviate words if you like, and the handwriting is not terribly important.

What *is* important is to keep a spiritual record of the time you are spending in prayer.

And then to review the record from time to time.

You will find that this prompts new reflections all the time, and prayers about things you wouldn't otherwise have thought to pray about.

It isn't easy to discipline yourself to do it, unless you

naturally enjoy writing. In fact, it is probably harder than the discipline of prayer itself.

But it is very rewarding.

John Wesley kept a prayer diary. It fills several volumes.

One Methodist minister friend wrote this in *his* journal, when he was having trouble keeping up with his entries:

"Well, my hat's off to ole John Wesley. How he ever covered 225,000 miles, mostly on horseback, preached 44,400 sermons, carried on extensive correspondence, oversaw the fledgling Methodist Church, and still found time for daily entries in his journal I'LL NEVER KNOW!"

But the journal was a measure of Wesley's spirit— or the Spirit that was in his spirit.

Over and over again on the same day, he talks about praying. Preached at one little town and prayed as he rode to the next. Had tea with a poor family and prayed. Went to lunch with a local minister and prayed. Preached and prayed as he rode on. Had tea again and prayed. Wrote letter and prayed. Preached in the late afternoon and prayed as he rode to a hotel. Had dinner and prayed.

The man was a praying fool.

Or a genius of a Christian.

The secret of a journal is the delight you take in making a record of what you have felt and experienced. You might put in something like this:

Had the strangest impression as I was praying today that old Mrs. Arden down at the end of the lane was in some kind of unusual need. Prayed for her, asking God to supply whatever it was. Later, after lunch, decided to walk down and look in on her. She has had the flu since the day before yesterday, and no one there to look after her. Fixed her some soup and sat with her while she ate it. Told her about the prayer. "My mother was right," she said. "How is that?" I asked. "More things are wrought by prayer than this world dreams of," she said.

Or like this:

Rode to Arbuckle today with my son and his girl friend. I was squnched up in the back of the Vega. Lay down across the seat and tried to meditate. The tires going over the lines in the road made such a bumping noise I had trouble. Then remembered reading that you can adjust to a regular rhythm and say a brief prayer to it. Decided on "Lord Christ" and said it over and over. "Lord Christ, Lord Christ, Lord Christ, Lord Christ, Lord Christ. . . ." Was wonderfully relaxed, and seemed to feel the presence of God in Christ dwelling in my life. Must remember to tell Bill about it for when he's driving alone. Or would it be too hypnotic? Don't know. Anyway, a good experience.

Or, on a bad day, perhaps something like this:

Had trouble praying today. Felt depressed and lonely. Judy was leaving for six weeks and I knew the house would feel empty. My back ached when I had been kneeling only a few minutes, and I was afraid I was going to have another pinched nerve. I guess some days are like that, God. I'm sorry!

Always be honest about your feelings and emotions. Don't let the desire to sound good to yourself lure you into writing things that aren't so. That would negate the whole purpose of the journal, which is to give you perspectives on yourself and your prayer life.

Don't worry if there are more negative entries than positive.

Or if most of them sound rather dull.

Your eye will always fall on the one that doesn't.

"Golly," you will think, "that was a great moment! I'm glad I had that experience. I would have forgotten it, too, if it hadn't been for my journal."

You will learn even from your more critical entries. Like this one, adapted from a friend's journal:

Thomas Merton speaks of the "desert place" as the abode of contemplative prayer. But how can God come in silence if I am not silent? How can he fill my empty place when I have not emptied it? How can love surround me when I run from it? "Be still . . . and know that I am God." Lord, help me to make a silence in the desert place of my soul.

But on occasion you will thrill to see that you have written something like this:

Cannot begin to describe the mingled sense of awe and ecstasy I felt while praying today. Very unusual. Had been reading Paul's letter to the Ephesians, chapter three, and meditating on each phrase and verse. When I came to the one that says, "To me, though I am the very least of all the saints, this grace was given," I felt very strange and light-headed. I kept repeating the verse. Maybe seven or eight times. "To *me*," it says. "To *me*." It was as if I were in the presence of God and all the angels, and Mozart was playing everywhere, or the *Hallelujah Chorus*, and I had no sense of time passing or anything! It was wonderful!

It is important to make an entry every day, just as you pray every day.

And don't worry about its being a fancy notebook.
One from the dimestore will do very well.

It is what you put in it that will make it valuable!

❧⫷ Conclusion ⫸❧

THERE IT IS.

A little introduction to the techniques of praying.

I hope you will find it useful, but do not take it overly
seriously.

Techniques are only techniques.

It is the presence of God you are really after.

"Mettez-vous en la présence de Dieu," St. François de Sales
invariably began his meditations.

"Put yourself in the presence of God."

That is what you are after. The rest is straw.

If you could do it by standing on one foot and cocking
your head to the sky, that would be wonderful.

If any of the things mentioned in this book are useful
as means to an end, I am glad.

If not, please do not stop looking. Prayer *is* real. It
is worth learning. Don't let this little book put you off
the track.

In looking back over the book, I am struck by one
thing. That is, how many of the techniques have to do
with the unconscious mind.

I am impressed by that. I think it is right.

There is much more to us than our egos, our conscious
minds, our rational beings. We are dreams, emotions,

fears, anxieties, hopes, loves, hates—all kinds of noncompressible, nonanalytical things.

And if we are to belong to Christ, then we must belong to him entirely, below the level of consciousness as well as above it.

We know that now, in an age of psychology. Though of course Christ, who drove out demons, knew it then as well.

Therefore prayer must spill into all of life, and all of life must get into our prayers.

There must be no holding back.

Everything belongs.

Our nervousness.

Our agression.

Our sexuality.

Everything.

God can handle it. We needn't fear to be honest before him.

It is *ourselves* we are afraid of, don't trust, endeavor to deceive.

That would be laughable if it weren't so true.

If we can just get through that barrier—the barrier of the self—life will be what it was meant to be.

God is waiting.

And it is *prayer* that will get us through.

Don't give up until you've made it!